POOR GABRIELLA

POOR GABRIELLA

A Christmas Story

By VICTORIA FORRESTER

with illustrations by

SUSAN SEDDON BOULET

& calligraphy by

JOHN PRESTIANNI

ATHENEUM · 1986 · NEW YORK

Atheneum
Macmillan Publishing Company
866 Third Avenue, New York, NY 10022

Calligraphy by John Prestianni, Berkeley, California
Printed and bound by South China Printing Company, Hong Kong

10 9 8 7 6 5 4 3 2 1

Library of Congress Cataloging-in-Publication Data

Forrester, Victoria.   Poor Gabriella.

SUMMARY: Recounts in rhyme how Gabriella, a cow,
was locked out of the barn at the Nativity.
[1. Cows—Fiction.   2. Jesus Christ—Nativity—Fiction.
3. Christmas—Fiction.   4. Stories in rhyme]   I. Boulet,
Susan Seddon, ill.   II. title.
PZ8.3.F76Po   1986   [Fic]   86-3607
ISBN 0-689-31265-2

For my beloved godparents,
Danica and Joseph.
–V. F.

For my father, whose memory
lights this book.
–S.S.B.

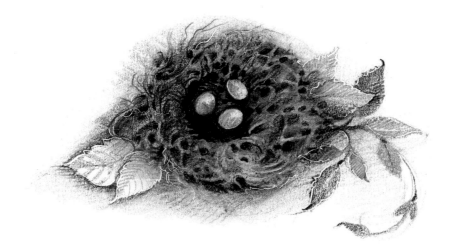

IT was a night
when all the stars were shining—
one brighter than the rest.
The night was clear and cold,
and angels sang,
but there were few who heard them,
for it was cold, frozen cold,
and doors were closed and bolted.

A shuffling noise was heard
outside the manger door,
hooves pawing the frozen ground.
"It's poor Gabriella,"
the animals said one to another.
(You will remember that on Christmas Eve
the beasts can talk.)

"Late again," said the sheep.

"Always late!" said the goats.
"And the barn door closed and locked."

Outside, the old cow stood shivering.

"Warm straw, sweet straw,"
bleated the lambs.
"Poor Gabriella."

"The cow needs me,"
thought the child
who was sleeping in the straw.
He opened his eyes beholding his hands,
warm as straw, sweet as straw,
but helpless as flowers in the manger's lap.

The sheep were warm,
the donkey fed,
but the old cow, come too late,
was cold and hungry and afraid.

The baby lying in the straw
could hear the angels
and he knew the stars by name,
but he could also hear
the shuffling in the night
and he could see the old doors
closed and locked – poor Gabriella.

"She needs me now," thought the child.
His hands opened like stars,
yet beholding his hands,
small and helpless as flowers,
he wept.

At the sound of his tears,
there awoke in the night
a Great Wind.

The walls of the manger shook;
the sleeping parents woke;
and, thinking that he too must be afraid,
the mother, so beautiful and so tired,
reached for the child to comfort him.

"This wind has no compare,"
she said to her husband,
"It is sudden and strange.
Look! How the wall trembles!
And the doors—might they not fly open?
Even the lambs are hiding themselves
in their mother's wool."

But Joseph looked only at the door.
"He hears," thought the sheep.
"He hears," thought the goats.
It was so,

and now Mary heard too.

"Dare I open the door?" he asked.
  "Dare we not?" was her soft reply.

"Warm straw! Sweet straw!"
bleated the lambs
as the cow was brought safely inside,
Joseph's mantle around her.

In peace
the wind ceased and withdrew.
And bestirring the air
where the young child slept
was a fragrance
sweeter than all roses.

Written out in the winter of 1986,
the hand chosen for the text
is a chancery italic,
based on 16th century
Italian models.